# Bluenose

2

## Tatiana Tomljanovic

**Weigl**

Published by Weigl Educational Publishers Limited
6325 10th Street SE
Calgary, Alberta  T2H 2Z9
Website: www.weigl.com

Library and Archives Canada Cataloguing in Publication

Tomljanovic, Tatiana
            Bluenose : Canadian icons / Tatiana Tomljanovic.
Includes index.
Also available in electronic format.
ISBN 978-1-77071-576-9 (bound).--ISBN 978-1-77071-583-7 (pbk.)
            1. Bluenose (Ship)--Juvenile literature.  I. Title.

VM395.B5T64 2010              j387.2'2              C2010-903744-8

Printed in the United States of America in North Mankato, Minnesota
1 2 3 4 5 6 7 8 9 0  14 13 12 11 10

072010
WEP230610

Editor: Heather Kissock
Design: Terry Paulhus

Weigl acknowledges Getty Images, Nova Scotia Archives, Corbis, Alamy, and CP Images as image suppliers for this title.
Roué Family Archives/JOELRO: page 11; Photograph Knickle's Studio & Gallery: page 9.

Every reasonable effort has been made to trace ownership and to obtain permission to reprint copyright material.
The publishers would be pleased to have any errors or omissions brought to their attention so that they may be
corrected in subsequent printings.

We acknowledge the financial support of the Government of Canada through the Canada Book Fund for our
publishing activities.

# CONTENTS

# What is *Bluenose?*

*Bluenose* is the boat shown on the Canadian dime. *Bluenose* was a fishing and racing boat. It was built and launched in Lunenburg, Nova Scotia, in 1921. The story of *Bluenose* has an important place in Canadian history.

CANADA 1993 10 CENTS

# Why was *Bluenose* Built?

In the early 1900s, fishers along the east coast of Canada and the United States each felt they had the fastest fishing boats. In 1920, they held a race. The United States won. The Canadians wanted to be sure they would win the next year. They began building a new boat. It was called *Bluenose*.

# How Did the Boat Get Its Name?

"Bluenose" was a nickname for sailors. Sailors would wear blue mittens when at sea. The mittens would leave a blue mark on their nose when they wiped it.

9

# Who Designed *Bluenose?*

An **architect** named William J. Roue designed *Bluenose*. He was a gifted ship designer even though he had no special training. William studied the features that made boats fast and put them into his design for *Bluenose*. The sleek, narrow boat could slice quickly through the water.

# What Type of Boat Was *Bluenose*?

*Bluenose* was a schooner. Schooners are sailing boats with two **masts** and large sails. Wind fills the sails and pushes the boat across the ocean. *Bluenose* had eight sails. They were attached to the **main mast** or the **foremast**.

**STERN** The back end of the boat is called the stern.

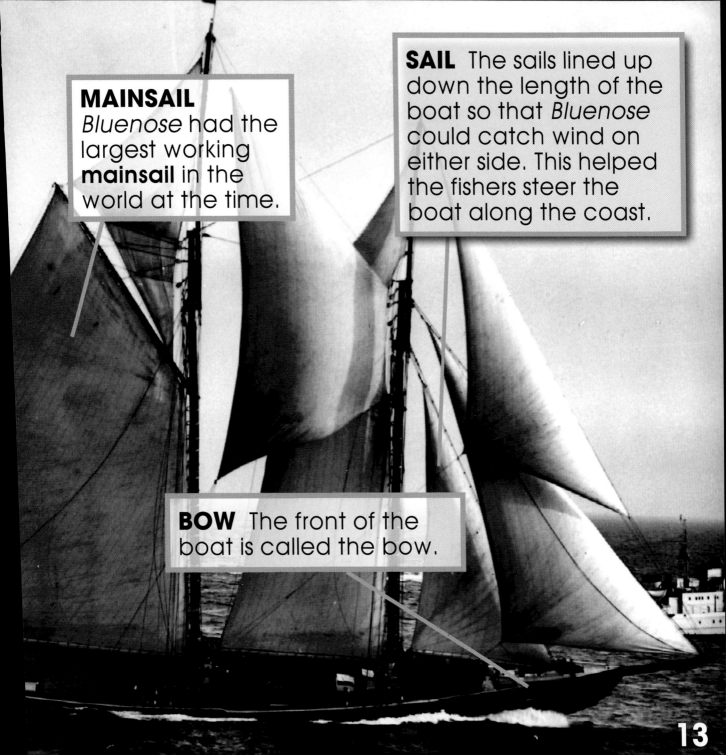

**MAINSAIL**
*Bluenose* had the largest working **mainsail** in the world at the time.

**SAIL** The sails lined up down the length of the boat so that *Bluenose* could catch wind on either side. This helped the fishers steer the boat along the coast.

**BOW** The front of the boat is called the bow.

# Who was the Captain?

Captain Angus Walters was given the job of **commanding** *Bluenose*. Walters came from a family of fishers. *Bluenose* was used for fishing when it was not racing. Captain Walters remained in charge of *Bluenose* for almost 20 years.

# A Winning Boat

*Bluenose* won almost every race it entered. The boat's last race was in 1938. By then, *Bluenose* was old. It was worn down. Most people did not think *Bluenose* would win. *Bluenose* proved them wrong and won the race.

# What Happened to *Bluenose?*

By the 1940s, *Bluenose* was no longer useful as a fishing boat. In 1942, the owners of *Bluenose* sold the schooner. She became a **freighter** in the Caribbean Sea. *Bluenose* sailed the Caribbean waters for four years. Then, she hit a **reef** off the coast of Haiti. *Bluenose* was shipwrecked.

# What is *Bluenose II*?

In 1963, a Nova Scotia family built a boat just like *Bluenose*. They asked William J. Roue for his help. The boat was named *Bluenose II*. The family sold *Bluenose II* to the province of Nova Scotia for one dollar. Today, the boat travels to special events, and people can take rides on it in summer.

# Make a Sailboat

scissors

milk carton

glue

string

paper

straw or stick

hole punch or
sharp pencil

small box to place
inside milk carton

1. With an adult's help, cut the milk carton in half lengthwise. Shape the ends of the milk carton with your fingers to bring both ends of the boat to a point.

2. Punch a hole in the middle of the small box with a hole punch or sharp pencil. Glue the box into the centre of the milk carton.

3. Cut out a square piece of paper about 1/2 to 3/4 of the length of the straw or stick. This will be the sail. Decorate the sail with paint or markers.

4. Punch a hole at the top and bottom of the sail. Weave the straw or stick through the holes. Wrap a string around the top of the straw, and tape each end of the string to each end of the boat.

5. Put your boat in an outdoor pool or in a bathtub filled with water. Watch it float along the water surface.

# Find Out More

To learn more about *Bluenose,* visit these websites.

**The Bluenose Legacy**
www.bluenose2.ns.ca/
Legacy/HistoryoftheBluenose.html

**Bluenose History by the Minute**
www.histori.ca/minutes/minute.
do?id=10213

**The Bluenose,
a True Canadian Champion**
www.tourcanada.com/
bluenose.htm

**Bluenose—A Canadian Icon**
www.gov.ns.ca/nsarm/virtual/bluenose/
default.asp?Language=English

# Glossary

**architect:** a person who designs buildings and ships

**commanding:** controlling

**foremast:** the first mast at the front of the ship

**freighter:** ship used for carrying cargo or goods

**main mast:** the tallest mast on a ship

**mainsail:** the biggest sail on a ship

**masts:** tall poles that hold up the sails of a ship

**reef:** a ridge of rock or sand just above or below the water's surface

# Index